PUSHING THE BOAT OUT

NEW POETRY

Edited by Kathy Galloway

First published 1995

ISBN 947988 74 2

© 1995, The Authors

Cover picture 'The Pilgrim Ship' by Mark Ianson, 1992.

Published by Wild Goose Publications

Wild Goose Publications, Unit 15, Six Harmony Row, Glasgow G51 3BA

Wild Goose Publications is the publishing division of the Iona Community. Scottish Charity No. SC003794. Limited Company Reg. No. SCO96243.

Distributed in Australia and New Zealand by Willow Connection Pty Ltd, Unit 7A, 3-9 Kenneth Road, Manly Vale NSW 2093.
Permission to reproduce any part of this work in Australia or New Zealand should be sought from Willow Connection.

A catalogue record for this book is available from the British Library.

Printed by The Cromwell Press, Ltd, Melksham, Wilts.

Contributors

Nancy Somerville

Ruth Burgess

Jess Kerr

Ron Ferguson

Yvonne Morland

Alyson Hallet

Catherine Orr

Kathy Galloway

Robert Davidson

Jan Sutch Pickard

Sheila Hamilton

Stuart Barrie

Ruth Harvey

Jackie Roddick

David Osborne

Liz Knowles

Contents

Introduction

Pushing the Boat Out seems like an appropriate title for a collection of poetry, especially one with its origins in a magazine called 'Coracle'. A poem is rather like a small boat launched upon a wide sea. Where it will go is anybody's guess, what it will carry to its eventual destination is equally unknown. If from these poems readers of this book receive some pleasure, some insight, some new way of seeing, the hopes of those who have launched them will have been more than fulfilled.

Almost all the poems published here are previously unpublished. Some are by established writers (though not necessarily writers of poetry). For others, this is a first venture into the unpredictable sea of exposing their work publicly. And exposure is not too strong a word; in writing to discover one's emotional truth, there is inevitably an element of risk, of vulnerability. One's boat seems very small, the sea very large, and even to attempt it a kind of impertinence. Beside the beautiful tall ships, there is a shrinking from what can feel like the vulgarity, the foolhardiness, of a tiny paper boat.

And yet, there is something to be said in favour of the attempt. Poetry, like music or art, is a human right, no less than the right to freedom, justice and the wherewithal for survival. And although life is sustained by breath, bread, shelter and the chance to work, the *good* life comes through what we care about. Expressing what we care about may come through our attention to loved ones, through political and social engagement, through our various faiths. But it may equally come in a song, a painting, a prayer, a poem. The denial of that expression is a denial of part of what it means to be human. That the suppression and constraining of artists is a tactic of totalitarianism is not therefore surprising. The small boats make it possible for us all to be braver in the small ways that most of us need most.

The themes which emerge in these particular poems are familiar ones. From most of the writers there is a strong sense of geography, whether that be well-loved or well-remarked places, or the equally interesting interior spaces that we seek out markers for. Not surprisingly, in a book published by the Iona Community, several poems are about Iona, and

others are about Camas – the Iona Community's adventure centre located in a remote fishing station on the island of Mull. There are poems about people, including two written about George MacLeod – the founder of the Iona Community. Many of the poems reflect the struggle to find a language that expresses a contemporary Christianity, a gospel and a faith incarnated in everyday life, engaged, as the Iona Community is, with a desire for and commitment to justice, peace and the integrity of creation.

The writers in this anthology have all arrived here by virtue of being connected in one way or another with the Iona Community, either as members, volunteers, or because their work has previously been published in 'Coracle'. This, however, is not the reason their work is included, but simply how it came to my attention in the first place. It's included because I like it! The other slightly unusual feature of this book is that, rarely for poetry, the women contributors considerably outnumber the men. This is not the result of any conscious bias or intention, though it is worth noting that most poetry anthologies are selected by men.

I would like to thank Tom Leonard for his encouragement and interest in the book. The image selected for the cover – 'The Pilgrim Ship' by Mark Ianson – was a source of inspiration. I thank him for allowing us to use it.

Kathy Galloway
Glasgow, September 1995

NANCY
SOMERVILLE

Nancy Somerville, born in Glasgow, is a Community Education Worker. Her poems and short stories have been published in various magazines and anthologies. She is an Associate of the Iona Community and worked at Camas, the Community's centre on Mull, in 1992.

Wild Geese Flying South

I watch the dark skein swerve and wheel
and return to its purpose,
each bird defined
against a misty grey sky.

The rain stained glass
and traffic noise
keep me from their calls,
and I feel apart
from life itself.
Rhythms and drives
are sanitised and commoditised,
rituals removed
more and more
from root and purpose.

The outstretched necks
and curves of wings
are living shorthand messages
for those, like me,
without direction,
left behind
to the hard shoulders and cold hearts
of a lost people.

Climbing with Tommy

– Just over the next ridge,
  Honest,
I lie.
Again.
But his six-year-old legs aren't persuaded
any more
by bribes of Rolos
and promises of views right over to the island,
where we camped a year ago.
– Remember the man who broke his leg
  playing at football with us?
  And him being lifted up
  into the helicopter?
  And the way it hovered?

The distraction only works
till his sodden feet complain
and we're stuck
while he sits
stubborn in the mud.

– Look at the snow.
And we're off again,
racing to reach the patches of white,
and I don't even mind when he stings my ear
with a direct hit.

Then the last last ridge
and he wants to know
– Will we really see Arran?

At the summit
it's hard to say where mists end
and clouds begin.
I'm blinded by disappointment,
but Tommy sees clearly and shouts
–   We're in the sky!
    We're in the sky!

Home Ground

She does not yield easily
to sight seeing
or picnic lunches,
her moods being viewed,
more often than not,
through a vague smirr
or a haar
floating like ghosts of fishermen
past windows set in stone.

She seeps through goosepimpled skin,
insinuates airways,
permeates veins,
and creeps into bones
until you're part of her.

The spirit stirred on Saturday terraces
rises in the sap of rowan and gorse.
But caught in your throat
an indefinable loss
which echoes along her shores
with the oystercatcher's lament.

Your pulse is the ebb and flow
of pride and disillusionment,
the aimless lapping
of hope and regret.

To Kendra

When I was young
the lark rose on its song,
trilled out of sight,
and I was
daughter
sister
grandchild in white angora.

When I was young
the water's edge boiled with tadpoles
eager for jam jars
and I had parents
illusions
all my teeth.

When I was young
old old people died
and children in countries far far away,
and guilt was for
an unwashed face
a broken vase
a cross-my-heart lie.

Around the corner
when I was young,
endless fields
a boundless loch
all the time in the world.

Because She Cares

Each day
God the Mother walks with me.

She holds my hand
at busy crossroads,
reminds me to be careful
because it matters to her
what happens to me.

She points out rainbows
when my mind is busy
on the deluge of paperwork
impatient on my desk.

She smiles at me
through friendly eyes
and with a blackbird's song.

God the Mother
walks with me
and my heart skips along.

Comfort

Ask me about comfort
and I'll tell you of a room,

of an old, slatted door
holding its own against a healthy wind,
by the rusting strength
in its rattling metal latch,

of a shuddering, salt-cornered window,
reflecting leaflets on times of tides
and the occasional bus to the ferry,

of damp, whitewashed walls
that leave their mark
on your top layer of woolly warmth,

of newspaper-stuffed boots
snuggling up to a peat fire
that glows your face to a flaming red
but leaves your back cold shouldered,

of steaming socks and dripping trousers
hung over fishing-net twine
slung from a soot blackened ceiling,

of a room filled
with the comfort of acceptance.

We Are

```
We  are          different
             one different
         all     different
We  are  all     different
         all                  people
             different people
We  are  all     different people
    are
We       all one            people
We are                nt
         one                people
              if
We  are              rent
              if
We  are              nt
              rent
We  are   one            people
      all one            people


We  are  all one different people
```

RUTH

BURGESS

Ruth Burgess, having survived youth work, teaching, community work, unemployment and working for Social Services, is currently preparing, after a gap of 25 years, to resume life as an irresponsible student, and is looking forward to every minute of it!

For Adam

who was very busy in Edinburgh
on a warm sticky afternoon ...

It is a fact worth knowing that if
you are four years old and you lie on
your stomach and stretch out your
hand into the water

you can just reach the coins that
sentimental adults have thrown into
the Waverley's fountain pool ...
Can't you Adam?

It is also true that most adults are
too hurried or too amused to stop
you ...
Aren't they Adam?

However, you need to remember, that
if your big brothers spot you and rat
on you,
and if your mother catches you,
she'll make you empty your pockets
and throw them all back ...
Won't she Adam?

Descent of the Spirit

Winter brought you a new beauty lady
Edging with white the hems of your garment
Showering your stars with snow.

Caught, like us, in the stillness
At one with the frozen earth
You await again the birth
That will bring us running
To greet your son.

Credo

Today has been a restless day
things going wrong in all directions
and my anger rising
at others
at circumstances
at myself.

God, you are in the midst of this
I sense your presence
prowling like a tiger
pushing me
pursuing me
restless yourself until I change.

I am ready to let rip
to hurl stones into oceans
to pound my fists into a brick wall
I am ready to shout
to rip sheets into shreds
to curse the darkness
to bury my head into warm flesh and sob.

I am afraid, God
that there is no one here but you and me
my friends are out or busy or far away.
Do I trust you enough to give you my anger, my loneliness?
Do I believe you enough to reach through the emptiness
and grasp for your hand?

Credo
God, I love you,
I can say no other words.

Poem for Hannah

One shoe off, one shoe on
sat on a quilt
smiling
catching the eyes of those
who sat around you
clutching at your mum's legs
mostly retaining your balance
occasionally tumbling.

We adults were listening to stories
that hinted where Jesus could be seen.

In the days after Candlemas
I saw him sitting in our midst
growing up in a little girl
one shoe off, one shoe on
and full of wonder.

St Queran's Well, Troqueer

This is a green place
trees, thistles, nettles
a place of power
a place to go barefoot
a place of prayer.

Here yellow leaves float and dance
bubbles surface and burst.

This water is cold
clean cold
stone cold
pure cold and holy
The earth's warmth shivers here.

This is a place of meeting
a whole place
a place of healing.

Celt of water
Christ of earth

touch me
wash me clean
and keep me in holiness
through my nights
and days.

Pontefract

Across the fields they loom
shivering, steaming
'cooling towers' my mind says
'monsters' my imagination whispers.
Always in the distance
never coming nearer –
but they might … !

Eric

If there is a good way to die
you had it Eric
dying as you'd lived
with Pat at your side
in a house where
your chair sat by the fire
close to the garden where
squirrels played and birds sheltered
near to the chapel
where you'd sang and thought and prayed.

What went on under that flat cap
who knew
maybe the children guessed.
What came out was smiles and stories
rarely sadness, sometimes anger.

Yours was a world where
the earth ran through your fingers
and fruit blossomed and ripened
to fullness
and was either eaten
or fell to bring strength back to earth
nothing wasted
nothing losing its worth.

On a cold December morning
we sang for you Eric and we sang loudly
for you are one of the saints, about to join the angels.
And we loved you
and we will miss you.
We will miss you with an ache of loving parting
as the rain comes down and the sun shines
and the leaves grow green.

Tabgha[1]

Jesus
you had a birthday today.
A little boy stood at the front of the church
and solemnly set alight
every stub of candle
that he could dig out of the sand tray
beneath your picture

And growing in the stillness
gloriously reflected
in your golden halo
and in his dark eyes
there was light, dancing.

1 Tabgha is the site of a church on the edge of Lake Galilee,
   where tradition supposes that a small boy brought bread
   and fish to Jesus.

In Your Nineties

In your nineties I met you
lover of sweet puddings
using your sticks to play ball
at floor level, with a crawling child –
your eyes and the child's meeting,
and twinkling with shared delight.

Of the George[1] of history I had read
I had heard the stories
the floating wood, the High Street E.
the glory of your prayers
shaking me into action and praise.

Yet the George I knew
was the old man
alert and passionate and obstinate still
whose failing body hurt
but whose loveliness,
childlike and mischievous,
still shone through.

1   *George MacLeod (1895-1991) was the Founder of
the Iona Community.*

A Conversation

'Who's buried there?'
a three-year-old voice
asked from the back of the tombstone.
'Sharon's little girl,' I said
digging into the sunken grass
and turning it over.
'Why is she dead?' he asked
'Somebody hurt her,' I answered.
'Like somebody punched and kicked her?'
'Yes,' I said
'I don't kick my friends at nursery,' he replied.

'I might get a spade for Christmas,' he said
eyeing up mine for size.
'You might,' I answered.
'What's it for?' he said
pointing to the new turf
as I measured it along the grave.
'Like a blanket,' I suggested.
'To keep her warm?'
'To keep her warm,' I agreed.

'I'm not dead,' he said
'No – you're alive,' I told him
'What's alive?' he said
'You can walk and shout and see ... and talk,' I said.
(You can also ask hundreds of three-year-old questions
that are making me smile
I thought – but I didn't tell him.)

I slapped the turf down and we poured
the water into it
watching it bubble and disappear.

Beginning to tidy up
I poured out
some stale water from the vases
'That's water that smells,' he said.
I agreed.
Then together we examined three dead slugs
that had drowned
and now lay bloated on the new grass.
'You'll have to clear them away,' he said
and I did.

JESS

KERR

Jess Kerr was born in the shadow of, and was later married in, Govan Parish Church. Her work with Community Education brought her back to the South West of Glasgow. Jess retired early to start writing. At present, she is involved with the new Glasgow Central Theatre Company.

Exchanging Places

Wrapped in the shadow of the arches,
begging forgiveness for being there.
Her fingers pinched the bow,
and tip-toed select strings
bestowing soulful music
on early morning sunshine.
'John Anderson my Jo, John,
We clamb the hill thegither ...'
Places changed in Exchange Place.
A trio on chair arms secure,
listened and learned in accord
as mony a winter's evening, Dad,
we sang wi' ane anither.
Big Issues swam in the glare
past Princes Square.

Remembrance

In step. Adrenaline pumps to pageant's drum,
November's breath fingers their frames, still they throng,
toes tapping, feet stamping, they're pushed, they push on.
'Old soldiers never die.'
They march.

In step. Women resolute, bosom held high,
Fought shoulder to shoulder or bravely stood by
to raise new generations and mourn and ask, why?
'Keep the home fires burning.'
They march.

In step. Eyes Front! Trust your comrades hold.
In welded embrace, three in step face the foe.
Eyes Left! If you've eyes left ... 'Much further to go?'
'There's something about a soldier.'
They march.

In step. To attention, this is their day.
Two minutes, a hot meal, a chat, and away,
to the glory you fought for. Four walls. One more day.
'It's a long way from Tipperary.'
They march.

R O N

F E R G U S O N

Ron Ferguson is a former Leader of the Iona Community, and is now the Minister of St Magnus' Cathedral, Kirkwall, Orkney. He is the author of several books including Geoff: The Life of the Rev. Geoffrey Shaw (1979), Grace and Dysentery (1986), Chasing the Wild Goose: The Iona Community (1988), George MacLeod: Founder of the Iona Community (1990), Black Diamonds and the Blue Brazil: A Chronicle of Coal, Cowdenbeath and Football (1993).

MacLeod the Seer

That half-cocked eye searches
me in quizzical mode,
defying, defying.
Its look is humorous,
with a hint of murder. (The kind
which pacifists can only dream of.)

You would write my life,
would you?
Of course you can try

to cross into no man's land but
the trench is deep and
corpses are stinking on singing wires and
there are unexploded mines,
mind you.
Of course you can try
to make me remember
(of course you can try)

says the eye, winking
and glinting friendly furious
in the fading sunlight.

That private public eye has seen
into the ghostly past – don't
linger there for Christ's sake –
and on into the present, tense:
has dwelt on horrors
and trembling moved to vision
a new thing, desperate.
No eye for an eye is this
which has seen the glory

of the coming of the Lord,
has learned to fear that terrible swift sword
which stabs awake at night.

And when the ferryman comes with ropes of pain
and blocks and tackle –
not still the red boat of MacBrayne? –
the hooded far-seeing jewel stays open,
half, watchful and controlling.
A hundred years in thy sight
are but yesterday when it is gone, O Lord
MacLeod of the ever watchful pupil,
who neither slumbers nor sleeps.

Behold Your Man

He stands his ground – and even yours –
deploring damning roaring ranting
and says (thank God) it's all for love
of Christ (but not His holy mother
if you understand).

His howl is howled (should it be fluted?)
as he wades the bloody river
there is nothing muted in this Captain
Furious. His aye is for an aye, his nay
means never; strong his right arm to smite
luxurious ease, his bullish face set hard
against deceitful Catholic charm
and weasel Southern comfort.
The wages of sin is death, is death;
there will be No Surrender.
The sash his father wore
is made of heavy chunks of mail,
a binding Orange armoured suit
of lore which makes him mobile
as a clanking Goliath –
invulnerable to slings
and arrows of outrageous
truth – or a lumbering Craigavon centre half.
When that day comes,
he will be lifted
high on luminous white steed,
drawing all men unto him. All roads will lead
to Paisley in the Irish unfree state.

The Taoiseach twitches at the Liffey bar.
Asked what he really thinks, he orders
a united Ireland (but in a whisper,
with a wink) and tries to laugh
when he is served a Bloody Mary. Blessed art thou
among drinks, the bearded barman quips,
crossing and double-crossing himself
with enigma. The smile which plays
around the tender's lips is taut,
the cocktail-maker's eyes as cold
as northern seas. He knows his pay day
has come close, he's counting now,
his tips have bought the wages of Sinn
Fein, as sure as death: while earnest crimson
bishops sweat in holy fury day and night
(for the love of Christ and his virgin mother)
to cleanse the green and pleasant land
of condoms.

Along the gloaming border road
the bleeding crosses bleed
and bleed and bleed.

And in the city still strung high
with lights and fading messages of peace,
goodwill, red-handed magi ride the Falls
on death-white steeds to meet apocalyptic fate
in 1690 on crumbling gable walls – Veni, veni,
Immanuel. Even now come late, come late –
while from the appointed tenement room
come shrieks of hell and fits of desperate loss.
Blessed art thou among bloody
women, the sardonic midwife spits
with the sign of cross in bitter theatre.

For the love of Christ! the Shankhill
schoolgirl howls, too often battered
and abused to be a holy mother. She bleeds
and bleeds and bleeds and labours
to bring forth a baby, blue
red blood-lines on his palms. Behold
your man, a tiny Protestant equipped
with stigmata.

Y V O N N E

M O R L A N D

Yvonne Morland was born in Wigtownshire and spent the second half of her childhood in Ayrshire. She has always felt herself to be a poet, although has ostensibly been a social worker (now lapsed). She completed an art course in 1990-92 and spent a year working on Iona in 1993. She describes herself as itinerant, growing and wanting primarily to make connections. She now lives in Edinburgh.

Pushing the Boat Out

Pushing the boat out adventurously
was never something I did easily;
incremental adventure was more my style.

Until I hit the biggest brick wall
and there it was – the chasm.
It wasn't really that I plucked up courage
to jump
simply, that I couldn't stay
teetering on the edge.

Crossing that gap was like
a prolonged scream
that even yet, echoes inside me.

It wasn't so much jumping
as stretching, reaching out,
e-l-o-n-g-a-t-i-n-g;
letting go only bit by bit
and dangling in mid air
for endless moments.
Reaching the other side
made me feel sick
and I collapsed in exhaustion
for a long time.

At the beginning of this journey
(was it the beginning?),
I wasn't even offered a boat!
'Walk on water,' I was told,
lovingly perhaps,
but there was no mistaking
the command.

Reaching across chasms
suddenly seemed easy.
Then there was,
'Don't be afraid,'
that's what claimed me;
that piercing connection
with the deep fear inside.
That was when I knew
I'd been recognised.
That's also when I knew
that the thing I wanted most,
the loving recognition,
would make me face the biggest test of all;
the biggest letting go.

It's been pretty stormy out on that water
ever since,
with surprising bouts of calm.
I never quite skim the waves
but some days, only my feet become submerged
and it almost feels like paddling.
Other days I'm thankful for arms
to keep me afloat
and not just my own.
Sometimes I'm there keeping others afloat;
paddling by their side
or letting them stand on my shoulders
to keep their feet out of the water
lapping round my arms.

It's a wide sea
and the horizon keeps shifting
but dry land doesn't beckon me any more
except in flashes.

I think the olive branch I'm looking for
would be a sign of something
other than land
but that's for another day
when I've learned more.

Meeting the Poet

The bright-eyed girl
braced,
colt-like,
nostrils lifted to the salt wind
blowing from a far-off shore,
feet planted firmly in the rutted turf
of her birth land.

Her words shout,
'I'll race ye!'
and she's off running,
laugh curling round your ears
and slapping your legs
into action.

And you leap dykes
and splash through burns
up to yir oxters
wi nae thocht
but tae follow.

The Whole Truth

I have to write
have to carve out
these agonies in my soul,
sing of the wild joys
my heart rings out
to the dank air, bending
into the far distance and off
into the night.

Response to a Friend

I have not put you on a pedestal,
there is no need.
You are there, a mast
to which I gladly pin my colours
when there is reason;
another precious broken reed,
companion in the current.

But if a pedestal is what you want,
I will fashion one of alabaster
or of clay if you prefer.
I will even help you up
if you desire to stand aloft.
I will put you out of reach
but will not remove you from my heart.

When

I

When I am tempted to forget
When I am tempted to forget You,
The earth tips wildly on its axis
And the seas roar through the crack.

The voice stills
And there is terror in the silence.
All is hollow, echoing.

II

When I remember
When I remember You,
Gentle tempests roar,
The crust of the earth delights to move
And trembles in the leaf.

The voice speaks
And there is clarity in the silence.
All is resonant, ringing.

Paradox

We are omnipotent,
able to order and destroy
according to our design.

Yet the turn of a leaf in morning sun
and the catch in our throat
drives us to our knees
and into prayer.

The Calling

Under a waterfall shrouded in night
Under a silvery moon
Out from the depths of silence she comes
Out of the depths of the womb.

Stalking the trails of the lizards she runs
Stalking them into the dark
Stalking and pausing and sniffing the air
Sensing the life in the spark.

Over and under and round them she runs
Over and under and out
Out to the clearest space under the sky
Wheeling the heavens about.

Round in a circle the heavens she spins
Round in exuberant joy
Sparking the tips of her fingers and toes
Rolling the world like a toy.

Rhyming she rings like a bell in the night
Clear on the crystalline air,
Follow her into the depths of the night
Follow her home if you dare.

A L Y S O N

H A L L E T

Alyson Hallet is a full-time writer living in Bristol. She has recently completed her first book of short stories and is currently working on a multi-media production involving dance, narrative, music and film for the Arnolfini Arts Centre. She has worked as writer in residence for Avon Poetry Festival, The Small School, Devon, and Shirehampton Library.

Childhood Flashback

From the movement of feet
clad in large socks
rubbing up and down
against each other

to the flash of friction
sparking through your body
streaking your mind
with terror

to sheets of naked light casting
shadows on days when you slept
with strife, bed linen stained
with misplaced desire

from the pillow tears fall
into the pit of security
that safely put locks
on the wrong side of doors.

Kabul on the Television – '91

Young boy vomits blood
sees camera sings
us a song 'one by
one the petals fall'

His thigh fits in circle
of finger and thumb
lips held tight
with smile of death

Children wake old
limbs of women grow
cold, amputated,
men pull tears, triggers

Empty shrapnel full
bellies groan
bloody fingers clasp
shredded flesh close

In the shells
of heart and home
cries of leave
us in peace.

Eau Sauvage

After he died
I cleaned every room, cupboard and surface
in our house.
I used April fresh, lemon fragrance, forest glade.

When I finally sat down to rest
and lay my head upon the kitchen table
I could still smell
Eau Sauvage
from the day years ago
when he knocked the small glass bottle over.

Sometimes I imagine splitting the atom
only to find a fragment of his voice inside.

Memory Collectors

Here above Bath's autumn valley
we search for goodbye
as cloud shadows shuffle across hills
and blacken the once blue deck sky.
In our thin hearts we dress
as kings and queens feverish
for new land, people and pleasure.

It starts to rain. Parched earth releases
the sweetest smell, tempts us to stay.
But we are bound by tickets and dreams
and an emptiness we never admit.
Standing to go we embrace, make promises
we know we'll never keep.

The king presses his good eye
to the telescope and focuses forward.
The queen bakes memories
hard as pebbles then polishes.
All around our minds she makes
a shiny moat that no boat or innocent
fool may cross for months to come.

CATHERINE

ORR

Catherine Orr lives in Glasgow where she works as a physiotherapist. To her surprise she was forced into writing poetry eight years ago by a sudden visit from a very insistent muse. Since then she has had her work published in various magazines and was a member of Bread and Circuses – a performance group. She is a mother and grandmother, and after three years of widowhood has recently remarried.

Aros Moss, Kintyre

Farms of the Moss
grey and enigmatic,
no trees or hills for shield,
you merge into the landscape.
Even your barns are camouflaged
like the huts and hangars of the Base.

Forlorn on the fields
buildings gathered about you
safe from ambush, but wary.
Windows keep watch for invaders
across a maze of little roads.

Who would visit you there
in that No-Man's Land
between the water and the hills
scarred by wire and watchtower,
the sound of the sea
like a distant battle,
and, closing in above the waves,
a NATO bomber lumbers home.
Not for you the honeysuckle,
fragrant on sunlit walls,
stark you stand, battle ready.

Small Demo

Death stakes its claim
marks perimeters
fences Faslane.
The grid's graph
dissects landscape.
Mountains and a sleeping loch
disintegrate behind meshed steel,
and we, like crows,
who build their careless nests
on both sides of the fence,
accept.

Death stakes its claim
knows no perimeters,
the fence at Faslane
protects us from nothing
but the truth,
hazy behind meshed steel,
and we, nest-building fools
on both sides of the fence,
have no resort.

Death stakes its claim
marks a side road
'To the cemetery, Faslane!'
'The cemetery is here,' you said
'Behind meshed steel!'
Flowers were bought
and with your engineer's hands
unused to tender stalks
and pliant tools
fashioned on the gate
and through the wire
a healing cross of daffodils.

Suburb

The gardens of Pollokshields
spread and slope
to the infinitesimal crumbling
of sandstone.
Peace settles beyond shrubberies
long undisturbed.

Do not explore.
Tigers may prowl by night
and sometimes watch in the afternoon
the woman weeding the path.
Sun through rhododendron leaves
strikes stripes that camouflage,
and certainly a fox was seen
to saunter on the lawn.
Eggshell fragments, turquoise, speckled
tell of magpies' cruelty.
Strewn feather and bone
are best ignored.

I rake the leaves
into mounds,
place damp clumps
in plastic bags,
find pleasure
in earth's funeral smell
and a stillness that encompasses
the city's fret and thrum.

Glasgoing-On

So they're smartening-up Dalcross Street.
The trottoir on my way to work
boasts glazed brick,
but the not-so-young man
stills courts the sun,
topless
at lunchtime
on the step.

Pigeons still sashay in posses.
Two cats licking Kit-e-Kat
all smug, paws curled
shoot fishy looks
from window sills
dining alfresco.

Yes, they're smartening-up Dalcross Street,
though stubborn puddles reappear.
The bony crone
whose knowing glances
tell me she fancies
I'm no better
than I should be
now in carpet-slippers
trains her squatting setter
to heap his faeces
in the gutter.

Tom Boy

She used to be the star
the leader of the gang.
They were always at the door.
Was she coming out to play?
Older than the rest
and a big girl for her age,
she managed them,
they towed the line.
She ran the show,
their heroine.

On the other side of teens
she's lost that impetus,
passive, she allows
others to rule the roost.
Did she spend herself too soon?
Has she already had the best?
Is she ill?
Is she in love?
Or did some frosty zephyr get her
blow its chill onto her Spring.
Blight her burgeoning.
Cut her down
below her size?

KATHY
GALLOWAY

Kathy Galloway is the editor of 'Coracle', the magazine of the Iona Community. She is the author of a number of books of poetry and theology. She lives in Glasgow.

The Line

Because I love you,
I will draw a line between us,
and over this line
I will not go.

Beyond the line,
in the space which is around you,
and which is yours,
lie your decisions,
your responsibilities,
your promises,
your power.
Yours, not mine.

Beyond the line,
if you struggle, I will not help you,
if you are sad, I will not comfort you,
if you are attacked, I will not rescue you,
if you are lonely, I will not be your company.

I will not weaken you,
shield you,
divide you from yourself.

Because I love you,
I will not cross the line to save you.

And if, encouraging from the other side
I see you look towards me once too often,
I will turn, and walk away.

Because I love you.

The Line Too

But there is also this:
though I will not always agree with you,
I will always take you seriously.
If people speak ill of you in your absence,
I will say the good I know of you.
And though my weeping for your pain may be silent,
my delight in your accomplishments will never be.
Sometimes I will play around the line,
like a cat,
twisting in and out of unravelling wool,
And sometimes I will push hard up against it,
and if you are doing the same,
we will be very close;
as close as breathing.

And if, by chance, I should meet you in the street,
then a shiver of delight will race through me like the
hot silent shriek of ecstasy,
melt my casually cold-stored heart,
and leave me smiling at the great good fortune
that put us on the planet
at the same time,
and made our paths to cross
when we could, so easily,
have missed each other.

Because I love you.

Cross-Border Peace Talks

There is a place
beyond the borders
where love grows,
and where peace is not the frozen silence
drifting across no man's land from two heavily-defended
entrenchments,
but the stumbling, stammering attempts of long-closed throats
to find words to span the distance;
neither is it a simple formula
that reduces everything to labels,
but an intricate and complex web of feeling and relationship
which spans a wider range than you'd ever thought possible.

The place is not to be found on the map
of government discussions
or political posturing.
It does not exist within the borders
of Catholic or Protestant,
Irish or British,
male or female,
old or young.
It lies beyond,
and is drawn with different points of reference.

To get to that place,
you have to go
(or be pushed out)
beyond the borders,
to where it is lonely, fearful, threatening,
unknown.
Only after you have wandered for a long time
in the dark,
do you begin to bump into others,

also branded,
exiled,
border-crossers,
and find you walk on common ground.

It is not an easy place to be,
this place beyond the borders.
It is where you learn that there is more pain in love
than in hate,
more courage in forbearance than in vengeance,
more remembering needed in forgetting,
and always new borders to cross.

But it is a good place to be.

Wired-Up

When a tremor shakes the ground
and the walls crumble away,
all the connections are laid bare
that run unseen through the house.
There are, of course, many of them,
making this work, and that work.
They are functional, strong,
mostly taken for granted,
not what are normally thought of
as very beautiful.
So it's a shock to touch them
and find them live,
vibrating,
carrying a thousand impulses,
powerful, electric charges.
This is why they're usually
embedded in walls.
It's safer that way.

Still, it's good to be reminded
from time to time,
that they're there,
that they're vital,
that silently
the wires are singing.

Prize-Giving

'Daddy, Daddy, can we go faster than them?'

I am planning to offer a prize
for the person who comes in last

the one easily   distracted
by the interesting
                    things
                        along
                            the
                                way
the one who stopped to talk
idled
by
the roadside
lifting her face like a sunflower

the one who stilled her breathing
            to keep pace with
            elderly gentlemen
            and the slow rise
            of the moon

the one who noticed the pulse beating
beneath the tanned woman's skin
and forgot where he was going
for several minutes

the one who got lost

> and found himself
> admiring strange architecture
> and smelling fish and oranges
> up an alley

thehighadrenalinesoakedthrillofgoingsomewherefast
is not to be compared
with the low-down pleasures
o f   b e i n g   s o m e w h e r e
s   l   o   w

I am on a mission to convert the world
I shall be offering prizes

A Time to Kill

Shall we kill some time together
you and I

murder a few clocks
neglect the radio alarm
sentence diaries to slow burning
or better
overcrowd them to extinction

hopelessly confuse annual events
by holding them according to the whims of toddlers
and making every day a birthday

shall we organize commuters to attack the railway timetables
diverting every train to Upper Largo
condemn the House of Commons to interminable MPs
throw wasted time off cliffs and re-examine the economy
pay everyone the same, so we can do away with
hourly rates
overtime
human resources management

We'll amalgamate youth and age
grandmothers will kick up their heels
and virgins will all be wise
plastic surgery will shrivel up and die

Of course, we wouldn't kill it all

We'll save the free time
We'll keep the good times

We'll have the time of our lives

A Time to Make

I want to make a little time for you

spin it out attentively
carve intractable blocks with alternatives
compose new variations on an old rhythm

give you the time I didn't spend running away

and if it's only a little time
and if it's a little rough around the edges
perhaps it will seem more to you
since each moment is big with worlds
of chance encounters
strong passions
easy silences
sea-borne ecstasies
and the timelessness of love

Camas Lullaby

Bracken and rock and rose-pink heather
will carpet the land for you.
Oystercatchers will dip and a heron
skim over the bay for you.
Bog-myrtle and wild mountain thyme
will scent the air sweetly for you.
Daisies and celandines and tormentil
will dance in white and gold dresses for you.
And the sea and the seals and the gulls
will sing an island lullaby for you.

(For H.M.B.)

ROBERT

DAVIDSON

Robert Davidson has had his work published by The Highland Printmakers Workshop and Gallery, Inverness, in a volume of poetry entitled The Bird and the Monkey (1995) and in 'Coracle', 'NorthWords', 'Chapman', 'Lines Review', 'Understanding' and 'Great Outdoors'. He won the Mountaineering Council of Scotland Article Competition in 1992 and 1993. He works in the water industry in East Ross.

Where God is Found

A ball rises until the force driving it up
exactly equals that of gravity and,
for a moment, hangs absolutely still.
A perfect sphere. In that moment,
that's where God is found.

An infant takes a few faltering steps
then looks up with a big two-toothed smile.
In that moment of looking up,
God's there.
And when the first of those teeth
split the gum. In that parting,
just there.

When lover eyes meet, God's there.
And when they unlock for good,
just before the first tear wells up,
and spills over the lower lid, yes,
there too.

You settle down with a book and
find yourself captured. That moment,
just before you realise,
is where God is found.
Round about page twenty.

Then, while you're reading, you feel
someone looking at you from behind and
you raise your eyes, all uncertain,
and look round.
Not when you turned your head,
or even when you had that feeling,
but when your concentration broke.
There!

A million million spermatozoa
cluster round an ovum so it looks
like it's coated in suede.
Suddenly one breaks through and
in that instant
the others fall away.
God!

Later when a two-cell egg
is tumbling down its tube
there comes the moment when
it adheres to the fallopian wall
and *implants*.
That's where God is.
And when it doesn't,
but tumbles on down and away?
There too!

In self-pity because
grief is mostly self-pity
and God knows all about grief.

Ever know something
but not know how?
How do you think?

In the cusp of a fingernail
and its growth at the quick.
In the turning of the furrow,
and the creaming of the bow-wave.
In the lift of the wing
and the angle of ascent.
God is decisive but elusive,
to be found in time
but leaving traces in space.

And where time and space are one,
there He sings his song of light.

Right here at the tip of my pen
a tiny metal ball
spreads dye across the paper.
Just at the point of contact God,
his robe bunched up in his hands,
is running like hell across the page.

Benediction

May all your hopes be sustained
Between the wings of seagulls
And may your fears before they start
Be taloned fast by eagles.

May curling salmon leap the falls
On the river of your strife
And pine trees crack with age
In the forests of your life.

May speckled fawns raise their heads
Beneath your vaulted blue
And may the God of frost and stars
Be evermore with you.

JAN

SUTCH PICKARD

Jan Sutch Pickard edits 'Connect', a magazine linking faith and action. A Member of the Community and mother of three children, she is a Methodist Local Preacher living in a small town in the Pennines and working in the centre of Manchester. She enjoys people, words, walking, worship and amateur carpentry.

Treading a Path

'A path may be built in Iona's twelfth century graveyard, to minimise erosion caused by visitors to the grave of the former Labour leader John Smith.' (The Guardian, Monday 25.7.94, which also contained the stories of Chimeme and Mary Cameron.)

Chimeme walks wearily
between the mass graves,
between the living looking for water
and the dying, lying down on the road.
It was a long road for her and the children
running away with the slow motion of a dream
among thousands of refugees.
'But we stayed ahead of the fighting
I thought here would be better because there is no war.
I never imagined we would have no food or water
or that we would have to walk so far.
It would have been better
if I had stayed in Rwanda.
It would have been a quick death there!'
Where her child died
the rock was too hard to bury him.
She wrapped him in his blanket
and left him there, far from home.

Mary Cameron
saw the death of her village, Inniemore,
one day in 1824.
'The hissing of the fire on the flag of the hearth
as they were drowning it
reached my heart,' she said.
When the home fires were out
there was nothing left for the people
but to climb the mountain
carrying their children

and their old people
and their few belongings:
refugees from the clearances
to the cities, to the colonies,
to an uncertain future,
cut off from community,
far from home.

At Garelochhead
a graveyard has been hijacked.
Who can read the names of the stones
which have been corralled
into the complex
of submarine pens, cranes
fuel stores, bunkers
and high wire fences?

These folk were buried
close to where they were born
and grew and lived and loved:
the barbed wire
has alienated them
stranded them far from home.

So folk are treading a path
to where a man with an ordinary name
is buried far from home
in a place that is open to all,
in a community restored,
in an island of peace in a world of war.
The angels said to the women
'Why do you search for the living
among the dead?'
But this is where we have to begin.

Chapel of the Nets

Remembered – left
at the back of my mind
like an old, closed, book –
a loft full of dusk,
nets, a gathered sense
of reverence and tradition.

But now we enter
a big echoing room –
a bare space
like a blank sheet of paper
waiting to be written –
open to become, in our hands,
a place of worship again.

Quarry/Query

Why
did the work stop
just then, just here?
The hillside sliced clean
to a ledge with one ruined hut.
But the rocks that were blasted
baring the land to the bone
are still stacked there,
or tumble into the bay
like a child's building blocks –
material for bridges
that have not been built,
for homes unhearthed
for churches unhallowed.
Red rock:
barren aftermath
raw material
unused –
Why?

Only these cottages
built firm as a fortress
facing the quarry across the bay;
where generations have lived
and laboured and died,
working the hill for the red rock,
working the waves for salmon;
where strung nets catch air and light
and fish are gutted on the stone,
meals made, fires kindled,
words and silences shared.

Sit on the doorstep,
quiet at the end of day,
gaze at the quarry
where one day
work just stopped –
with one last echoing blast –
leaving this desolation.
Imagine those building blocks
becoming bridges, homes and churches;
imagine poppies blooming
out of the red heart of the rock.

At Corrymeela

Opaque mist
translucent stones
unlocked by the sea
stolen by the sun.

Iona greenstone
comes from the furnaces
of creation;
saves from drowning –
so they say.

Stones on Ballycastle beach
come from broken glass
sea-changed;
symbols of reconciliation –
or simply hopefulness.

Building an Altar

It could be a single piece of marble,
hewn and carved by human hands,
or a cairn of stones
worn smooth by the jostle of the waves;
it could be a window sill, mantelpiece
or kitchen table;
it could be here – or anywhere,
outside or within;
it could overflow
with wealth or symbols and offerings,
candles, flowers, colour, creativity,
light and dark,
with icons, incense, starched white cloth,
the sound of bells, the taste of bread and wine.
    It could be blessed by all of these –
    and sometimes it is.

And sometimes it is stripped:
a bare board,
a hard place
without candle or colour.
or the rock is flawed,
cracked across
like a broken and contrite heart.
    But it can still be
    an altar.

Casting Off

The man in shirtsleeves
spits on his palms,
eases the hemp collar from a bollard
on which someone has painted a smiling face.

A lifetime of casting off –
you taught us
to relish such moments,
who spent restless years
moving on,
leaving one safe quayside after another.

This was one port you left –
patrolling the Western Isles,
skipper of a small air-sea rescue boat –
at this point I cross your wake.

But I am making my own journey,
restless, still searching for a harbour
which will also be
a point of departure.

The last time I saw you
was on another quayside,
leaning on your stick,
watching the men loose the mooring ropes,
watching us, children and grandchildren
growing smaller, waving, waving.

The man in shirtsleeves takes the looped rope
like a wreath and throws it across the space –
the dark water
growing wider all the time.

S H E I L A

H A M I L T O N

Sheila Hamilton was born in 1966, grew up in various parts of England and now lives in Edinburgh. She was the Abbey Guide at Iona in the autumn of 1992. She has had poems published in various Scottish and English magazines.

The Angels of God

(from the Carmina Gadelica[1])

'May the angels of God make smooth the road.'
I picture them there in the dawn and dusk,
in the loud rain, not ethereal or Italianate,

making smooth the road for the making
of justice. From the jetty to the abbey
they make it smooth, they heave away boulders.

They make the road smooth
for us to be just
in the places that aren't,
the stony places,
where the ill still have
their illnesses, the debt-ridden,
their debts, and the bailiff waiting.
May they tread there also.

1   Carmina Gadelica, recently republished by Floris Books,
    Edinburgh, 1992.

In Defence of the Political

'Can poetry be political?'
you pose, in your letter, rhetorically.
Meaning, I suppose, that it can't.

El Salvador may well boast
rivers that gleam in diamond sunlight,
jade-green trees aquiver with quetzal,
several sorts of gorgeous parrot,
sufficient colour, in fact,
with which to make a carnival.

But I can't be sure.
I know that in El Salvador
the Saviour is shrieking
and crying in the hedges.

Travelling into Romania After the 'Revolution'

In our bags, incongruous mix
of cocoa powder, contraceptives,
text books, and some nice bananas.
We share a cigarette, see
through the grey-filmed windows,
flat fields which could be anywhere.

Train stalled at the border,
the guards peer
at the absurd imperial splendour
of my navy, crested, Western passport,
search other people's bags
for anything possibly banned
in recent regulations.

The train draws out.
The tense, thin faces stay.

Vietnam Tropics

Reading an Article

Black words on white paper
yield cries and calls
send humming of birds
singing through the soul,

the every-now-and-then flutter
of some rare butterfly
on gorgeous pink petals.

Snub-nosed monkeys
rustle through thickness of trees,
the postwar generation.

crested gibbons call out
in the startling dawn.

South Africa After the Elections

On the day I was born,
someone got into the parliament
without being noticed
and stabbed in the back
Hendrik Verwoerd,
the man who made apartheid.

The summer I was ten,
seven hundred black ten-year olds,
in Soweto, died.

Between school and university,
people died in townships
with burning rubber round their necks.

And always, again and again,
that song they were not meant
to sing, that cut right through
my soul.

And I have seen Satan fall.

That song that cuts
right through my soul,
now, in the different world.

God bless Africa.

At the Time of Funerals

There has been dark before,
but not this dark,
clocks turned back,
winter come with a vengeance:

the fishmonger,
his pregnant daughter,
the couple who came
to town for curtains.

Such sorrow of God,
here,
and in all of the desperate places.

There have been dead before,
myriads of them,
but not these dead,
these gaps in the landscape:

the childhood sweethearts,
the old bespectacled man,
the man who walked miles
each day to buy milk
for the cats.

Such sorrow of God
for the sorrow of his creatures.

STUART

BARRIE

Stuart Barrie is fifty-one years old; born and lives in Glasgow; written poetry for over forty years; worked at Rolls Royce over thirty years; shop steward over twenty-three years; married over twenty-seven years; stopped drinking over twenty-three years; been searching over eighteen years.

Startled

Coming round the corner like that,
you startled my breath.
All that stuff from yesterday flashed up
stomach flips
smiles that caused bubbles
laughter like sex.

'Hello, you're looking well'
'Y-e-s ... yourself?'
'Yeah, you know, so so.'
Empty words to cover embarrassment
or guilt.

We parted, you spun and called
something I didn't catch
I couldn't turn,
my eyes grew enormous
walking on I whispered
'S'alright, s'alright'

You startled my breath.

Payment

I remember being sodden with pain
the kind of pain you can't treat with morphine
worse still, was the injustice of the suffering.

The space between the black floods would find me
raging with righteous indignation
an angry wordless roaring in my head
then wearied I'd slump back in the swamp
hot sobs shredding my helpless child insides.

And through all this,
not once
not even for an inkling
never
did I blame myself

I know better now.

Ally

You're my friend to the end
I'd swallow pride, hurt inside,
for you.

This is a promissory note I'm writing
a quill dipped in my heart wrote these words.

A part of me might die for you
and if it is only a small part
and if it is only a small might
it's me, not you, that's chained in a kennel
not a steel chain
not a real kennel
a chain of fear
a kennel of darkness.

But nothing is forever
I'm working on this
I've got a torch and hacksaw
I'm searching for batteries and blade.

Hang on,
I'm coming.

RUTH

HARVEY

Ruth Harvey is a probationary minister with the Church of Scotland, working and living in Leith. She is a Member of the Iona Community.

Wholly God

If God were a woman
I would be much braver
when it comes
to the heart of the matter;
or rather, when it comes
to matters of the heart.

If God were a woman
I would throw my inhibitions
to the wind.
I would sparkle
and toss and bounce
with laughter and the guts of love
as the sole means of
communication.

If God were a woman
life would be
as light as the top soil,
as free as the froth, or the frost,
which come and go with the seasons
and the tides and
make a slave of
no-one.

If God were a woman
life would be round and full
and tears would conquer fear
which would tremble,
then disappear
in the presence of
such splendid
wholeness.

If God were a woman
life would be complete.
Nothing more. No show.
No great crusade. No mission.
For God would be complete
in you, in me, that's all.

A Pattern of Prayer

For
each time of tension
each moment of question
each uncertainty
each hesitation
there was the lighting of a candle:
    a flame
    a flicker
    a space
    a vigil
    a waiting
    for the right time.

And then – and then
as each question is answered,
    each uncertainty faced
that pattern of prayer changes;
those symbols of healing
those votives of peace
    some gently
    some wildly
    some by a breath
        by a touch
            a stamp
    flicker. Fade.

And now – and now
as I stand in the smoke
amidst the glowing wicks
and the choking wax
waiting for the air to clear
I search for a flicker of light
as a candle of hope is lit for the future.

JACKIE

RODDICK

Jackie Roddick is a New Member of the Iona Community. She was living in Chile during President Allende's attempt to organize peaceful social revolution. She worked with Chilean refugees in Scotland and solidarity movements after the brutal coup of 1973.

Saint Columba

The Rule of Healing

Saint, seer and politician, he
beached Irish hearts along this scree,
a bubble of song, a lyric cast
for wind and source must change at last,
the last coast's fire lights up the lea.
Change is the Rule that follows the sea.

When you came, we were just fragments pooled,
Scot and Welsh and Pictish fools
colliding in surges and scrabbling for rule
one over another.
    Then you came, and threw us high,
building a wall between sea and sky
where monks could shelter and wise men preach,
Jew and Arab in easy reach.
One rock made community,
    Change is the Rule that follows the sea.

When you came, we had such expectations,
peace on the hills for generations
and Scots in the valleys. *All* of them. Aye:
and new building of churches:
    but the past settled slow,
the abbey oaks grew mistletoe,
the crosses, moons. And the Picts came by.
Saint of the oak grove, who taught us to see
pagan roots to the Trinity,
teach us to see it reach out and flower
in the life and voice of our enemy.
    Change is the Rule that follows the sea.

When you came, the world was in flux.
In the Far East the rains dried up
and the tribes tumbled westwards towards our coast.
Saxon kings laid Arthur's ghost.
We raised up heroes, and still we lost,
victory wanted, whatever the cost.
　　You brought their sons to be abbey reared,
We raised to manhood, the kings we feared
and found them friends. So let it be,
　　Change is the Rule that follows the sea.

Saint and seer, could you foresee
the bloody end of community?
　　Vandals in government over these lands:
　　Orkney to Dublin in Norse hands:
　　this abbey crumbled, these vows untied:
　　peace in ruins and justice denied!
Saint of the war band, surely you see
grief cries to heaven for remedy!
　　Change is the Rule that follows the sea.

I see Scots forced eastward towards the coast
joining the Picts; and a monk at Arbroath
calling his people to sovereignty
over powers and kingdoms. I see
new life, nation, identity
in the gift of the pirates.
　　I also see
Gael chiefs selling their land for sheep,
the fires in the valleys fall asleep
and my poor fragment peoples hurled
to loot and plunder the wide world.
　　Change is the Rule that follows the sea.

I see a new time when the rains may fail,
the sea winds blow a desert gale
and the world's peoples come to the core
choices to be made between agreement and war
on the back of that bitter legacy.
    I see Norse at the centre trying to bind
the wounds with what arguments they find,
I see Norse lives spent to make the world one,
Hammarskjold, Palme, Gro Brundtland's son.
I see love and anger, but no enemy.

Saint, seer and politician, he
beached Irish hearts along this scree,
a bubble of song, a lyric cast
for wind and source must change at last,
the last coast's fire lights up the lea.
Change is the Rule that follows the sea.

Cornelia's Song

From Acts 10, and in memory of Helena Zarrur

I remember when, down that bus-ridden road
too near the Palace,
you, borrowed angel, lighted in my flat:
bare mattress, tin of mackerel, head of curls,
Argentine dancer and
culinary skills of diplomat,
fit feast for sacrifice,
one of Allende's girls.

You, who had no wise way with men.

And Pallas Athene came,
authoritative and stern,
to lay down Law and Lenin: she
for whom those Palace walls
one day would burn.

I remember when you took me, a stranger
and that other bitter exile, hand in hand:
flesh of slave and sense of danger
with flesh of centuries of alien rule.
And sang, *No somos los extranjeros,*
Los extranjeros son otros,
los son los mercaderos
y los esclavos nosotros;[1]
and Christmas came, in a cheap glass of wine,
from you, who had no wise way with men.

And Pallas Athene came,
authoritative and stern,

to say that liberation never was
an exile with a girl at home:
she for whom factories
one day would burn.

I remember when, my borrowed angel,
you brought them home in handfuls:
compañeros lost, division-tossed, complacent too,
to sew their self-inflicted wounds
into a quilt of opinion just too short
to smother the coming coup.
You, who had no wise way with men.

And Pallas Athene worked
long bitter nights, with arms
to shore up hosts and make the boundaries sure: she
in whom the people's hopes, this century,
were now secured.

I remember when we had news of your death,
in our far Glasgow winter:
how soldiers came to pluck a journalist,
and you
who could have turned the Andes in their bed
and killed all you had kissed
had held them with your breath upright,
your contained breath.

You, who had no wise way with men.

And Pallas Athene lives,
miraculously, still stern
preaching not liberation but
some other social gospel: she
for whom two decades back
the city's poor heart burned.

And I, who would Athene be
for very pride
must set authority aside, and learn
from you, my borrowed angel,
gently to stitch man to man
into a patchwork pattern wide enough
to smother Nature's coup.

For people of bus, plane, private car –
all Gentiles without the Law –
and soldiers too.

From you, who had no wise way with men.

1   From a song by Daniel Viglietta.
    'We are not foreigners.
    The foreigners are other people,
    those who would buy and sell us
    and make us slaves.'

DAVID

OSBORNE

David Osborne has been writing occasional poems and songs since he was nine. He has worked in the construction industry in Edinburgh, studied engineering, theology and education, and taught secondary school in Somerset and Nigeria. He has been an Anglican Minister since 1980, working first in the Midlands and currently in a group of villages in Somerset.

Country House

No cottage, this one,
in a row of buff and brown,
four roofs, eight doors,
privet, and mud,
space for the pick-up,
the rusting maxi
and Brian's truck;
crisp bags in the wallflowers,
dog and chain at the woodshed,
three cats and two saucers
by the peeling door,
a leaning clothes post
and jeans on a sagging line.

Nobody's dream,
but somebody's home.

Village

This is our world:
the hedges speak to us
of our childhood's games,
and the trees of our courting.
The school took our children
and the churchyard our husbands.
Our neighbours know us,
friends advise us,
there are babies to hold
and groceries to buy,
jobs to do
and cousins near.
It is neither good nor bad.
It is ours.

Surprise

Sudden.
Sharp.
No dimming of light.
No lifted leaves.
No rolling echoes.
A few spots
on the bright window.

June rain.

And it is gone.

Oak Tree

Once the master;
now the watchman.
A thousand years of cultivation
leave you alone.

Once you were pillars and roof
of the lowland forest.
Now you stand barely proud
in a lake of cropped grass.
An elderly gentleman at the sea's edge.

But for the owl and the flycatcher
your are as you have always been,
and at your passing
the soil itself will mourn.

To Travel

For some there is always a reason
not to travel:
work
or growing weeds,
a wedding
or worried neighbours.
Staying at home must be easier
but how does the spirit survive?

Devon

Monument

It says that these hundreds who died,
gunned from a U-boat on a training exercise,
helped significantly the Allied cause
in its preparations for the liberation
of mainland Europe.

'How?' asked the boy.
And the man said he doubted if they really did.

Perhaps he was cynical.
But perhaps again
the government and the glorymakers
are unwilling to accept
that many deaths
are a pure
and simple
waste.

Edinburgh

Looking

Looking for tartan,
for history,
for a taste of Scotland,
spires,
wynds,
rock,
closes,
Stevenson and Mary Queen.

But look also in the bars,
the workshops and the tenements,
the hostels,
the new town precincts,
and among a million exiles
celebrating a homeland
they left
with hope and lament.

Brittany

Newspapers

Le Figaro.
Le Monde.
All you need to know
of the summit
and the election campaign,
the court cases,
traffic, sport,
television,
the economy,
the world.

Of Britain
nothing.

Reagan is going there.
McEnroe will play there.
What of importance is happening there?
Nothing as far as we can tell.

That
in itself
is worth remembering.

Brittany

Le déjeuner la vie

At noon the world stops
and eats.
At two it begins again.
At four and five
the world is alive.
At eight it slows down,
talks,
makes love,
and sleeps.

Somerset

Glastonbury

Dreams of once and future
in stones and crystals
and rainbow garments.

Shepton

Bargains round a market cross
awaiting another day
and a former glory.

Wells

Sandals and churning motors
through brisk trade
and a pageant of bishops' dreams.

Street

Once we crafted the world's shoes.
Now we sell
and hope the world remembers.

L I Z

K N O W L E S

Liz Knowles is an Essex Celt, born and brought up not far from Bradwell on Sea where St Cedd evangelised the East Saxons when he sailed down from Lindisfarne in his coracle. She now lives in South East London. A lifelong Anglican, she has always been involved in her local church. She works at Church House, Westminster, and besides writing, music and needlework, is a regular broadcaster on RTM Radio.

We Are Not of This World

we are not of this world
we
are not of this world
though feel we must

I think of you
exclusively
in a context of complete works,
that rounded,
that whole,
a definite shape
full as the moon,
pregnant with potential

we are not of this world
we
are not of this shadow
a part

I think of your depth
unknown fathoms
to plumb and dive,
and sink and swim
in glorious dark oceans
deep and rich as blood

we are not of this world
we
are not of the flesh
entirely

yet feeling in our flesh
I am emotion incarnate,
passion personified
feeling your every movement
your every mood

we are not of this world
we
so happy to be passing through
touching, momentarily, in time

Incarnatus

hour by hour
season by season
in the beautiful stillness
oh heart of my heart

can this be truth
in any recognizable form?
can this be a dream, a hope
made flesh?

if I dared to dream
I think it would be you
I saw there

Kisses Blown

If kisses blown could reach you
Tonight
There would be hurricanes
Touching your heart

Dust to Dust

come sit by me
as long as I have life
and love
come sit by me
once in a while
to remind me

as I walk the earth
I know one day
I shall be in the earth
I shall be earth
(tread softly, you tread on me)

come sit by me
as long as I have life
and love
come sit by me
once in a while
to remind me

Death is a Lonely Place

death is a lonely place
where others cannot accompany you
even those of us that love you
can only come so far
and then look on

death is a lonely time
of remembering
when chance words and objects
bring back floods of memories
and tears

did I tell you I loved you
did I ask you for all the answers you knew
and give you enough of me

death is a lonely space
of emptiness
where you were once a presence
a brightness in our lives
and we are trying to get used to
missing you soon

this death is only you
and however much we love you
and pray for and think of you
it is only you
that can do it.

(For Patti Evans, my godmother, died 20 August 1994.)

WordSong

I hear the heavy clouds gather
with angry hurricanes
thick with thunder
is this,
shall this be
your final word?

in the beginning
was the word

and I watched and waited
watched your lips move
waited
to feel the weight
of your vowels

you sang to me
solitary singer
before time was born
your voice rose
like more than an angel
there was brief stillness then

a thousand singers
could not bring me back your song
a thousand songs
could not retrace that one beauty

the memory
is not the song itself
the memory
is the beauty of it
I cannot forget
how beautiful
it all seemed then

I Walk Dangerous Paths

I walk dangerous paths
the line
between right and wrong
I am not always right
(I am not always wrong)
no parallel lines
these
they
converge in places
where boundaries are not defined
and
I dream
of arrival

OTHER TITLES FROM WILD GOOSE PUBLICATIONS

SONGBOOKS with full music (titles marked * have companion cassettes)
COME ALL YOU PEOPLE, Shorter Songs for Worship* John Bell
PSALMS OF PATIENCE, PROTEST AND PRAISE* John Bell
HEAVEN SHALL NOT WAIT (Wild Goose Songs Vol.1)* John Bell and Graham Maule
ENEMY OF APATHY (Wild Goose Songs Vol.2) John Bell and Graham Maule
LOVE FROM BELOW (Wild Goose Songs Vol.3)* John Bell and Graham Maule
INNKEEPERS & LIGHT SLEEPERS* (for Christmas) JohnBell
MANY & GREAT (Songs of the World Church Vol.1)* John Bell (ed./arr.)
SENT BY THE LORD (Songs of the World Church Vol.2)* John Bell (ed./arr.)
FREEDOM IS COMING* Anders Nyberg (ed.)
PRAISING A MYSTERY, Brian Wren
BRING MANY NAMES, Brian Wren

CASSETTES & CDs (titles marked † have companion songbooks)
Tape, COME ALL YOU PEOPLE, † Wild Goose Worship Group
CD, PSALMS OF PATIENCE, PROTEST AND PRAISE, WGWG
Tape, PSALMS OF PATIENCE, PROTEST AND PRAISE, WGWG
Tape, HEAVEN SHALL NOT WAIT† WGWG
Tape, LOVE FROM BELOW† WGWG
Tape, INNKEEPERS & LIGHT SLEEPERS† (for Christmas) WGWG
Tape, MANY & GREAT† WGWG
Tape, SENT BY THE LORD† WGWG
Tape, FREEDOM IS COMING† Fjedur
Tape, TOUCHING PLACE, A, WGWG
Tape, CLOTH FOR THE CRADLE, WGWG

DRAMA BOOKS
EH JESUS...YES PETER No. 1, John Bell and Graham Maule
EH JESUS...YES PETER No. 2, John Bell and Graham Maule
EH JESUS...YES PETER No. 3, John Bell and Graham Maule
WILD GOOSE PRINTS No. 1, John Bell and Graham Maule
WILD GOOSE PRINTS No. 2, John Bell and Graham Maule
WILD GOOSE PRINTS No. 3, John Bell and Graham Maule
WILD GOOSE PRINTS No. 4 (On the way to the cross), John Bell & Graham Maule
WILD GOOSE PRINTS No. 5, John Bell and Graham Maule
WILD GOOSE PRINTS No. 6 (Christmas scripts) John Bell and Graham Maule

PRAYER/WORSHIP BOOKS
THE PATTERN OF OUR DAYS, Liturgies and Resources for Worship, (ed.) Kathy Galloway
PRAYERS AND IDEAS FOR HEALING SERVICES, Ian Cowie
HE WAS IN THE WORLD, Meditations for Public Worship, John Bell
EACH DAY AND EACH NIGHT, Prayers from Iona in the Celtic Tradition, Philip Newell
IONA COMMUNITY WORSHIP BOOK, THE
WEE WORSHIP BOOK, A, Wild Goose Worship Group
WHOLE EARTH SHALL CRY GLORY, THE, George MacLeod

OTHER BOOKS
EXILE IN ISRAEL: A Personal Journey with the Palestinians, Runa Mackay
FALLEN TO MEDIOCRITY: CALLED TO EXCELLENCE, Erik Cramb
RE-INVENTING THEOLOGY AS THE PEOPLE'S WORK, Ian Fraser
ROGER, An extraordinary Peace Campaigner, Helen Steven
WAY TO GOD, A – A biography of George More, Mary More

THE IONA COMMUNITY

The Iona Community was founded in 1938 by the late Lord MacLeod of Fuinary (the Rev. George MacLeod DD). It was initially a movement for renewal in the Church of Scotland. The rebuilding of the ruined cloistral buildings of Iona Abbey (completed, through a combination of professional and voluntary work over nearly thirty years, in 1967) provided a powerful focus for the specific concerns of the Community: the integration of work and worship, politics and prayer, and the development of new forms of worship, of the common life, of youth work, of the ministry of healing, and of experiments in mission.

The Community today is a movement of some 200 members, 1,200 associates and 2,000 friends. It describes itself as 'an ecumenical community, within the Church of Scotland, of men and women seeking new ways of living the Gospel in today's world.' Its members are committed to a rule of daily prayer and Bible study, sharing and accounting for the use of their money and their time, meeting together, and action for peace and justice in the world.

The Community maintains three centres of work, worship, and the common life on Iona and Mull, and administrative offices in Glasgow.

Please complete and return to:
The Iona Community, Pearce Institute, 840 Govan Road, Glasgow
G51 3UU; Tel: 0141 445 4561; Fax: 0141 445 4295.

I would like further information about the Iona Community's work.
Please send me:
....   Membership details
....   A Deed of Covenant form
....   Information about volunteering on Iona
....   A catalogue of publications